A BALL'S GAME:

The Ball Talks

Stefan Mathis

A Ball's Game: *The Ball Talks*

Copyright © 2022 by Stefan Mathis

ISBN: *9781959449812*

All rights reserved. No part of this book may be reproduced or transmitted in any form or by any means, electronic or mechanical, including photocopying, recording, or by any information storage and retrieval system, without permission in writing from the copyright owner.

The views expressed in this work are solely those of the author and do not necessarily reflect the views of the publisher, and the publisher disclaims any responsibility for them.

To order additional copies of this book, contact:

Proisle Publishing Services LLC

39-67 58th 1st Floor Woodside

New York, NY 11377, *USA*

Phone: (+1 347-922-3779)

info@proislepublishing.com

Table of contents

Chapter 1 Introduction 1

Chapter 2 Getting A Ball 5

Chapter 3 Pre Game................................... 15

Chapter 4 My Game (July 12, 2014)........... 22

Chapter 5 2nd inning 37

Chapter 6 Innings 3 and 4 39

Chapter 7 Mid-Game.................................. 40

Chapter 8 The Stretch............................... 42

Chapter 9 Two Left..................................... 44

Chapter 01 Making A Big Splash 47

Chapter 11 Home Sweet Home................... 62

Introductions

Hi! What's your name? Where are you from? I'm glad to meet you. Well, today is the big day. Are you excited? I bet you are. I know I sure am. I can't wait for the game to start. I guess I should introduce myself. I am the Rawlings Official Major League Baseball or ROMLB for short, and I am the narrator of this story. My friends call me Bennie.

Where am I from, you ask? I'll be happy to tell you. In the big inning. Oh, wait! I'm getting ahead of myself. I'm really excited about the game, you see. I meant to say, in the beginning. The beginning of me, that is to say. I'm only one of the 2.2 million Major League baseballs produced each year.

I am the All-American kid. . . I mean ball. . . for the All-American game. Well not exactly. We (my friends and I) are actually made in Costa Rica. However, the parts all come from America. My center is a small rubber ball with a cork center (my heart) which comes from Mississippi. Yarn, twine, and string from Vermont. I start out as a small rubber ball. Then approximately one mile of string is spun very tightly around the rubber ball. This is done by machine to keep the string consistently tight.

Next, my shiny white cover is sewn around the string. My cover is made of leather from Texas, Oklahoma, and Colorado. The leather is tanned in Tennessee. My cover is sewn around me with 108 red stitches. This procedure can be done only by hand. It can't be done by machine. The human race can put a man on the moon, but cannot make a machine that can properly stitch a baseball. Go figure.

It takes approximately 20 minutes to make each baseball. It takes ten minutes to wind the string and be stamped with the MLB logo. Then the stitching process takes about ten minutes. After that, it takes a few hours for the logo to dry depending on the weather. Costa Rica is in Central America, south of Mexico, where the weather is usually hot and humid at the Rawlings factory. So, let's do some simple math. If we multiply 2,200,000 balls by twenty minutes for each ball, we get 44,000,000. Divide by 60 to get hours and that equals 733,333 hours and 20 minutes. My brain is hurting from all this math. Can we please change the subject?

Now I'm ready to go! Well, not quite. Due to the drying time for some glues used to secure the string to my center, I must spend another week in Costa Rica. Then I'm put in a box that holds a dozen balls. That's twelve balls if you weren't able to figure out the last problem. Four balls wide by three balls deep (4×3), or is it three balls deep by four balls wide (3×4)? My brain is starting to hurt again. Wait! I don't have a brain, just a heart. Remember?

Now my box, along with lots of others, will go to the warehouse awaiting our trip to the Major League Baseball stadiums in the United States and Canada.

A Ball's Game:
The Ball Talks

Getting A Ball

There are two ways to get a ROMLB like myself. The first way is to buy one at a store or gift shop. It might go like this:

Kid says to store clerk, "Sir, I'd like to buy an official Major League baseball."

Clerk: "Come right this way. Here they are, on the top shelf." The clerk hands the child a baseball.

Kid: "Mister, this box sure is dusty."

Clerk: "I don't sell very many of them."

Kid: "How much does it cost?"

Clerk: "Twenty dollars."

Kid: "That's a lot of money. Is there any other way I can get one?"

Yes, there is, kiddo. Indeed, there is. Remember me, Bennie? I'm the one telling this story. I mentioned there are two ways to get a

ROMLB. The second and most fun way is . . . . drum roll, please . . . . go to a Major League Baseball game. At the ball game, there are three fun ways to get your hands or glove on me or one of my friends. (1) catch a foul ball (fun). (2) have a real, live Major League player toss or give you one (funner). (3) catch a home run ball (funnest).

If you want to catch a home run ball, you need to buy seats beyond the outfield fence. Try to sit close to the fence to increase your chances of catching one. There are only a few home runs hit per game. In some games, none are hit. The best and funnest home runs are those hit by the team you are routing for. In some major league stadiums, home runs hit by the visiting team are thrown back onto the field. That poor ball will become tomorrow's batting practice fodder; carefully crafted and handmade, yet sent to the dungeon of batting practice. Oh, the indignity!

The next way to get a major league ball is to be handed or tossed a ball from a player. Lots of times this is done by the defensive player who records the last out of the inning. As the player leaves the field he usually tosses the ball into the seats. To get a ball in this manner, it helps to have the more expensive seats closer to the field. More often than not the player tosses the ball in the seats without regard as to who gets the ball. However, if you cheer and shout about how great a player he is, his toss may be directed more toward you. If you get a ROMLB in this fashion, treat it like a prized possession.

Now to add folklore as to how you came into possession of a genuine major league baseball, you should have a player autograph the ball after the game. On a side note, here's a story I heard while waiting to leave Costa Rica. There was once a young boy who borrowed his dad's autographed ball to play a baseball game at the sandlot with his friends. The ball had been autographed by Babe Ruth. If you don't know your baseball history, Babe Ruth was one of the greatest home-run hitters ever. That particular ball was possibly worth a fortune. If the player who autographs your ball ends up in the Hall of Fame, you could have some money coming your way.

Now let's talk about the most common way to snag a genuine major league baseball, namely catching a foul ball. In most games, foul balls are quite plentiful. There are two kinds of foul balls: the ones that stay on the baseball field and those which reach the seats where you watch the game. Little can be said about the foul balls which stay on the diamond except, "Mis pobres amigos," doomed to be tomorrow's batting practice balls. Mis pobres amigos is Spanish for "my poor friends." I learned that while down in Costa Rica.

What you are hoping and praying for is a ball hit toward your seat. My dear friend, please take note of the following important fact. I weigh 5.25 ounces and am very hard. There is a reason why catchers wear protective gear, batters' helmets, and fielders' gloves. I can hurt you if I hit you. That, however, is not my

A Ball's Game:
The Ball Talks

intention. I'm just looking for a loving home. You don't even have to feed me like that puppy you brought home from the pet store. And, remember don't let that puppy chew on me. I am a hand-stitched ROMLB and deserve to be treated with respect.

Here are some things to keep in mind when you see me approaching your seat. First and foremost, I'm coming towards you after being hit with a bat made of solid wood. Also, the person who hit me is a professional athlete with a lot more strength than a 10-year-old from the little league field. I could be coming toward you as a soft pop-up or a screaming line drive.

If I'm coming your way softly, or have bounced already, thus taking off some of my speed, you may be able to catch me with your baseball cap or maybe even your bare hands. If I'm a scolding hot line drive, use a glove or move out of the way. Most of the time the first person to touch me does not end up with me. Due to sheer surprise, speed, and ball hogs, whether you're holding a drink or a hot dog, getting me in your grasp is like trying to catch

a greased pig in a rainstorm. The one who finally lays claim to me needs to be sure-handed, fleet of foot, and just plain lucky.

There's one more thing to consider if you want to go home from the game with a new ball, and that's where should you sit. To almost guarantee, you'll leave the game with a foul ball you should sit somewhere along the first or third base side of the field. Consider where major leaguers hit foul balls. If he swings a little bit early, he will hit the ball behind him. If he swings a little bit late he will hit the ball in

A Ball's Game:
The Ball Talks

front of him. If he swings perfectly on time but hits me a little lower than dead center I will fly into the backstop behind home plate. I will then fall to the ground, be picked up by the ball boy or ball girl, and put in the batting practice bucket. If a right-handed batter swings too early he hits the ball down the third base side. When he swings too late, the ball goes toward the first base side of the field. With a left-handed batter, the opposite is true. Swing early, first base side. Swing late, third base side.

Having said all this, if I had my choice and the seats weren't sold out, I would sit somewhere along the first base side. Why, you ask? First of all, most people in the world are right-handed, including major league batters. Second of all, pitchers throw more fastballs than any other type of pitch. The faster the pitcher throws the ball, the greater the likelihood of the batter swinging late. So, a right-handed batter will usually foul the ball in front of him (first base side). This is the science of foul ball grabbing in all of its inaccuracy.

I hate being the bearer of bad news, but it is entirely possible to leave the game without that white and red globe of joy. But before you break down and buy that elusive ball at the stadium gift shop, let me give you one more option. Try MiLB. You say, "I just went to a Major League Baseball game and I didn't get a game-used ball. So now I guess I'll have to buy one." Let me say this to you again. Try MiLB. You missed the letter "i." What I'm referring to is Minor League Baseball. At a Minor League game, you get a ball the same way as a Major League game. Home run ball, foul ball, and schmoozing with the players.

A Ball's Game:
The Ball Talks

Here are a few facts about Minor League Baseball. First, there are more minor teams than majors, which means more opportunities to snag a ball. Second, smaller crowds equal more ball-hawking chances. Also, tickets to Minor League games are cheaper. This allows you to go more often. So give the younger guys a try. Some of them will be major leaguers one day. Just imagine an autographed ball by a minor leaguer who goes on to the Hall of Fame. You'll be able to say, "I knew that guy way back when." Remember the Babe Ruth ball.

Don't upset yourself over the idea of getting a Minor League baseball instead of a Major League ball. Are there any differences between the two? There is one: where they are put together. A Minor League baseball is made in China. However, both balls are made by Rawlings from the same materials from America. Same amount of string. Same cork center. Same leather cover. One hundred eight, you guessed it, hand-sewn stitches. A Minor league ball is stamped with the word "China" on its cover. This satisfies a trade agreement between the United States and China. Major league balls have no designation as to where they are made [Costa Rica].

A Ball's Game:
The Ball Talks

Pre Game

After my long journey from Costa Rica, I finally have arrived at a major league stadium. I don't know exactly how I got here because I was in a box, and it was dark. My box is put in the stadium equipment room. Many of my friends from Costa Rica are here. I see Bill, John, Mike, and Bobby. It's a big ROMLB reunion.

Hey, look! We are being moved and set on a table. Our box top is being removed. Ahh. . . fresh air and. . . ouch, ouch my eyes. . . bright blinding sunlight. Am I still at the Rawlings factory? Wait! Wait one second! That's not a real sunbeam burning my eyes. It's a sunburst logo on the wall. The sunburst logo of the Tampa Bay Rays.

I must be at the Tropicana Field in St. Petersburg Florida. This is the home of the Tampa Bay Rays. The locals refer to Tropicana Field as The Trop. In reality, it's never hot and sunny at The Trop because it's a dome stadium. I know what you're thinking. Baseball and sunshine were made for each other. That's true in most places in the country, but not necessarily in Florida. Due to Florida's lower latitude, the sun's rays and heat are very intense. If you suffered sunburn or heat stroke while watching a game, you might not want to come back.

The sun and the heat also results in water evaporation. Water evaporation forms clouds which turn into rain. Are you beginning to see a problem? In the early part of the game you'd get sunburned, then later, rained on. This is a miserable way to watch a baseball game. The sun and heat combination also leads to thunderstorms which often produce lightning. The Tampa Bay area is the lightning capital of the United States. All these weather elements would hinder an enjoyable game. Without a

A Ball's Game:
The Ball Talks

domed stadium, the Rays games would be frequently canceled due to rain or lightning. From June until late September it rains almost every day in Tampa Bay.

It's two hours before game time and the Rays equipment manager has moved ten boxes of balls to the umpires' dressing room. There are a dozen balls in each box. A grand total of 120 balls needed for today's game. Baseball sure uses a lot of math.

Just like the players and umpires, I have to get ready for the game. To do that, the umpires (the guys in charge) give each ball a rub-down. Every ball used in a game has to be rubbed with mud. This mud comes from the Delaware River. The mud is collected from a secret location in New Jersey. [Sounds confusing, I know, but if you look at a map you will see the Delaware River also flows through New Jersey].

This mud takes the sheen off my cover. A brand-new baseball is too slick for pitchers to get a good grip. A small dab of mud is rubbed on to my cover to make me a playable ball. The umpires hand rub each ball, carefully avoiding getting any mud on the seams. Mud on the seams will get a ball a trip to the batting practice bucket. Every game used ball or game ready ball for the last seventy-five years has been hand rubbed with mud. Some engineers and scientists believe that a machine could be made to mud rub baseballs, but Rawlings management and baseball traditionalists don't want to hear it.

The balls you buy in the gift shop are not game ready. They have not been rubbed and still have their sheen. Those guys are referred to as "pearl." Pearls are great for autographs, but those guys don't have the toughness to play the game. Who am I kidding? Whether a baseball ends up in a gift shop or on the field is just pure chance. The only difference between the gift shop pearl and me is those guys are individually boxed. One ball, one box, gift shop. Twelve balls, one box, field.

It is now my turn to be rubbed. I'm picked up by the home plate umpire and dabbed with a tiny bit of mud. A little goes a long way. Most Major League teams only use one or two buckets of mud per year. Each bucket contains two pounds of mud. Getting a mud rub is like exfoliating your skin. When it's done, you feel invigorated and ready to go. I'm ready to play ball.

There are four umpires working today's game. Rubbing balls before the game, making calls on plays during the game. Ten dozen balls will be rubbed for today's contest. That's ten times twelve (dozen), one hundred twenty balls. Divide one hundred twenty balls by four umpires and you get thirty. So each umpire has two hours to rub thirty balls. Better get to work boys. Time is ticking. No worries! It only takes a few seconds to rub a ball.

Let's do a little figuring again. You may want to get a pencil, a piece of paper, calculator, and a slide rule. I'll wait while you collect these items. Every year, Major League

Baseball gives every team 1320 balls completely free. There are thirty major league teams. Calculator ready? 1320 × 30 = 39,600 balls, and they all need to be rubbed. These balls generally are used for batting practice. In addition, each team buys three thousand boxes, each with a dozen balls for game use. Use only pencil and paper this time. Three thousand times a dozen. Don't you just love math problems? OK, 3000 x 12. The answer is 36,000. The final breakdown per team: 1320 free balls + 36,000 purchased ones, for a total of 37,320 per year. You might find this surprising, but a team only needs one or two buckets of mud to rub down all these balls. See, a little goes a long way.

With all the balls rubbed, the umpires go get dressed. We balls are left on the table, relaxing from our rub down. Soon the stadium equipment manager will pour my friends and me into that big box over there marked with a big letter R. What does the R stand for? You guessed it. Rubbed. Rub-a-dub-dub, balls in a tub box. Hey! This box is made of wood. . . hopefully from recycled baseball bats. That would be justice for what those bats do to us.

A Ball's Game:
The Ball Talks

Two strong ball boys carry the R box to the home team's dugout, in this case, the dugout of the Tampa Bay Rays. The Rays use the first base dugout. The home team may choose which dugout they wish to occupy. There is no rule about which side of the field a team has to be on. First base dugout is the home for eighteen Major League teams. The other twelve Major League teams have chosen the third base side. The R box is placed in the corner of the dugout against the wall. The box placement keeps us dry in case of rain. That's not going to happen here at The Trop.

From my seat in the box (or is it box seat), I can see the whole field. Allow me to go off on a short tangent. The seats closest to the field along the first and third base side are referred to as "box seats." Box seats are generally the place where a player tosses the ball as he leaves the field. Being closer to the players comes at a little extra expense. This extra expense is gladly paid by true ball hawkers seeking a little round treasure.

My Game
(July 12, 2014)

It's almost game time. I'm going to sing a song while you make your way to your seat. Don't forget those last-minute concessions. Okay, here I go... "It's a pretty good crowd for a Saturday, and the manager gives me a smile, for he knows it's me they been coming to see, to forget about life for a while." Billy Joel, Piano Man.

This applies very well for today's crowd. And, yes, today is Saturday. Baseball game attendance is at its best on Saturdays. With each team playing 162 games in seven months, that's a lot of Saturdays.

Right now the players are in the clubhouse getting dressed for today's game. Coach Joe is giving our guys a pre-game pep talk. Oh, sorry! You may not know about coach Joe. Joe Maddon is the manager of the Tampa Bay Rays. Our guys. Remember. We are here at

A Ball's Game:
The Ball Talks

Tropicana Field in St. Petersburg, Florida. Wearing white uniforms with blue trim are our guys. Those guys wearing grey on the other side of the field are the Toronto Blue Jays. Grey blue jays? Don't ask. It's a long story. A quick rendition of this story centers around the fact that there were no washers and clothes dryers in the visiting team's clubhouse.

As Joe finishes firing up the guys, I must listen to the General's instructions. "Who is the General," you ask? The General is the oldest ball in the R box. Don't worry about his age. We're baseballs, not eggs. We won't go bad. The General is a ball that was not used in yesterday's game. Yesterday's game did not use all 120 rubbed balls. There were a few other balls that wanted the General's position but did not have the qualifications. The General's position is based on the amount of time in the R box, and one's made date in Costa Rica.

Shh! The General is about to speak. "As you are all aware, I'm the General. So I'll be giving today's pep talk. Every one of you has a heart. And every heart wants only one thing. . . to find a home. You must find a way to get yourself into the hands of one of our adoring fans. We are up against two opposing forces: offense and defense."

"For the offense to send you home, you have to be hit with a bat. These bats are made out of northern white ash, a very hard wood. In the best-case scenario, you will only be hit once. You'll be hit as a home run or foul ball that goes into the seats. Some of you will be hit as a fair ball. As long as you remain a fair ball the umpires will keep you in the game. You will have to suffer being hit with a bat several times. After being knocked around for a while, pray that a batter will eventually hit you into the seats."

"This brings us to the group of balls that will suffer the most: you guys who are hit as foul balls that stay on the field. You will suffer a fate worse than death. There is no glory when you become a batting practice ball. No autograph on your cover. No place of honor on a trophy shelf. Quite the opposite, in fact. You will be beaten with bats every day until your seams bust."

"We were all purchased by the Tampa Bay Rays organization. As Rays balls, it's our obligation to do everything in our power to ensure a Rays win today. Here's what we have to do. First, we must allow ourselves to be hit by the Rays batters. When the Blue Jays pitcher tries to throw you fast, slow down a little bit. If the pitcher wants you to curve, make yourself a big curve, not a sharp one. On the other hand, when the Blue Jays are up to bat, you need to help the Rays pitcher. Make his fastball faster and his curveball sharper. Being in this R box since yesterday, I've seen what those Blue Jays bats can do. Don't allow yourselves to become a Jays game-winning home run."

"Let's talk about the defensive part of the game. The defensive players love us and want to protect us. They wear soft leather gloves on their hands to stop us from rolling on the ground. Even better, when we are hit into the air, they catch us before we fall to the hard ground. If they have a choice, they will work together to keep us in the R box."

"The pitcher is the head of the defense. He throws us toward the batter. He is trying to keep us from being hit by the bat. Sometimes he throws us fast. Sometimes slow. He can also make us curve to miss the bat. The pitcher has seven friends called fielders on the field with him. It is their job to keep us safe. One other guy, called the catcher, works with the pitcher. The pitcher and catcher are masters at ball and bat avoidance. These two use skill and trickery to keep balls from being hit. They hate to see a bat and ball collision."

"The pitcher, catcher, and fielders would like nothing better than a quiet hit-less game. No balls being hit all over everywhere. No one having to chase all those balls. No runs scored by the opposing team. As I wrap up this pep talk, I'd like you to remember one thing the most. Avoid the Jays bats! Now let's go have some fun."

Okay, kiddo! I'm back. Your friend, Bennie the baseball. The General gave us some good advice. Now the players are coming into the dugout. Each player chooses where he would like to sit while his team is at bat. At bat is the offensive part of the game. The players hit us with the bats. The players try to run to as many bases as possible after hitting the ball.

It's 4:10 pm. Game time. Joe has told the players to take their positions on the field. In baseball the visiting team bats first. The home team is on the field playing defense. The home team gets to bat last. A baseball game is divided into nine untimed periods called innings. Each inning has two parts: a top and a bottom. At the top of each inning, the visiting team bats and tries to score runs (points). In the bottom of the inning, the home team tries to score. The team with the most runs after nine innings wins the game.

The Rays are on the field doing their warm-ups. Warm-ups consist of each player throwing a ball around several times to each other. The pitcher generally tosses eight to ten pitches to the catcher. Meanwhile, the other team is getting ready to bat. Players put on their batting helmets and take a few practice swings.

"Welcome to Tropicana Field," we hear over the speakers from the public address system. "Today's game will feature the visiting, division-leading Toronto Blue Jays against your hometown Tampa Bay Rays. Immediately following today's game, the summer concert series continues. Performing all their hits will be Rock and Roll Hall of Fame inductee Joan Jett and the Blackhearts. Now please stand, remove your hats, and join in the singing of the national anthem."

"♪♪ . . . Oh, Canada. . ." Wait! That's not right. I know what you're thinking. You came to see America's grand game and the national pastime. So, what's going on? Allow me to clear the air. Because Toronto is a city in Canada,

A Ball's Game:
The Ball Talks

this is considered an international game. In these types of games, the national anthems of both countries are played. I hope Greece never gets a Major League baseball team. I hear their national anthem has twenty-seven verses. Some people will want to go home before the game starts.

Going off subject for just a minute, I bet you can't guess Canada's leading export. It's hockey players. There are a lot more Canadian hockey players than baseball players. I imagine that's because Canada is colder than most parts of the United States. It's a whole lot easier to play hockey on a frozen pond than baseball in the snow.

"♫♫ . . . Oh, say can you see, by the dawn's early light. . ." Okay! Here is our anthem. Let's sing along. "♫♫ . . . And the home of the brave. Play ball!"

Did you catch that last part? Here's an interesting fact for you. You may find this hard to believe, but most baseball fans don't know

"Play ball" is not part of the national anthem. Okay! That's not actually true. I'm just pulling your leg. Let's get back to the game.

"Batter up," yells the home plate umpire. "Now batting," says the game announcer. The game is beginning. It's the moment we've been waiting for. I don't know about the other guys, but I'm about to cry tears of joy. There are only two things I can hope for at this point. The first, and most important, is to be out of this box by game's end. Second, and my prayer, is to avoid becoming a batting practice ball. I hope I get myself into the hands of a fan who does not go home early. I really want to see the Joan Jett concert. "I love rock and roll. Put another dime in the jukebox, baby." You know the song.

My friend Kevin has been chosen to be the first ball used in today's game. Kevin and I were box mates. We've known each other since Costa Rica. That Kevin is one funny guy. The catcher signals the pitcher to throw Kevin as a fastball. Okay, Kevin! Remember the General's words. Avoid the Jays bats.

At this point, I should try to explain catcher signals to you. The catcher is the player crouched down behind home plate. His job is to catch every ball the pitcher throws, whether the batter swings or not. He is also in charge of defending home base (the plate). Not that kind of plate. Before every pitch, the catcher signals the pitcher what type of pitch to throw the batter.

The catcher dangles his fingers between his legs to signify which pitch is needed. One finger down means the catcher wants the pitcher to throw a fastball. Two fingers is the signal for a curve ball. Three fingers for some kind of off-speed pitch. An off-speed pitch is also known as a changeup, or change of pace. These are the three basic types of pitches most pitchers throw. The pitcher throws these at different speeds to confuse the batter.

The batter may think a fastball is coming but instead gets a slow changeup. So, the batter swings too early, fouling the ball behind him. Most any pitch not hit with near-perfect timing will result in a foul ball, or easily caught by the fielders.

When the batter, also known as a hitter, correctly guesses what type of pitch is being thrown, he will quite often be able to hit the ball. If you are reading this story, you probably are a real fan of the game, but maybe not an expert. Let me clear up a misunderstanding many people have. Hitting the ball with a bat is not a "hit." All baseball players from kids to major leaguers can hit the ball with a bat. In most games, the bats hit the balls many, many times. However, a "hit" in baseball lingo is

A Ball's Game:
The Ball Talks

when a batter hits a ball in such a fashion as to allow him to reach a base safely. The hit ball must touch the ground, or fence, or go over the fence in fair territory.

The pitcher winds up and releases the pitch. Here comes Kevin. He's a ninety-five-mile-per-hour fastball. The batter swings and misses. "Strike one!" yells the umpire. The crowd is cheering wildly. One pitch and the Rays fans can already feel a win coming. The catcher flashes two fingers. Kevin is going to be a curveball. As Kevin flies toward the plate, he should be making a sharp turn. He is not.

"CRACK" is the sound as the bat hits Kevin. He has been hit very hard. He's flying very high and far down the third baseline. Oh, no! Kevin is about to be a Blue Jays home run. No! No! He's going, going, going. . . foul. Wow! That was close. A fan wearing a Blue Jays hat caught Kevin. Everyone at the Trop is happy, including that Blue Jays fan at today's game because he has a new baseball.

For the game to continue, we need a new ball. Where around here are we going to find another ball? The R box, of course. Wait one moment. It doesn't work quite like that. The umpires do not run over to the R box each time another ball is needed. The home plate umpire is responsible for introducing new balls into the game. To keep him from having to walk back and forth from home plate to the R box 70, 80, 100 times per game, he gets help from the ball boys and girls. They bring him four balls at a time. The umpire wears a marvel of modern ingenuity around his waist that holds five baseballs. This marvel is called a "ball bag."

A Ball's Game:
The Ball Talks

Some non-baseball purists want to call it a "ball pouch." When the ump has only one ball left in the bag, the ball boy/girl brings the ump some more.

The next ball to enter the game is John. Kevin lasted two pitches, both strikes. The swing and miss fastball, and the long foul ball. Foul balls count as strikes. Some foul balls turn into outs, if they are caught in the air by a fielder. The pitcher winds up and releases the pitch. Here comes John. He's a curve ball. He breaks sharply, right into the strike zone. The batter does not swing. He was expecting a fastball. The ump yells, "Strike three!" That's one out and twenty-six more to go. I can smell a Rays victory. John continues his success by striking out two more Blue Jays. The Rays pitcher will get the credit for striking out the batters. But, we all know it was John who did all the work, avoiding Blue Jays bats.

Bottom of the first inning, Rays turn to bat. As the Rays come off the field, I hear Joe say, "Grab some wood, boys. Let's bust some balls."

But it doesn't happen. The Rays get no hits. John became one more strike out, before he was fouled into the backstop. Doomed to the batting practice bucket.

The Rays had two other ground outs, but no hits. They did, however, manage to foul two of my friends into the seats. Kevin, John and those other two guys--gone in the first inning. I didn't know those other two guys. They were in the R box since yesterday. The General is the only one left from yesterday's batch. I hope the General gets into today's game.

2nd **inning**

The top of the second inning was uneventful for the Blue Jays. Two ground outs and one infield pop-up. No runs, no hits. Three foul balls into the seats. Two foul balls stayed on the field. We know their sad fate. . . batting practice bucket. The bottom of the second for the Rays was also uneventful. They hit five foul balls: four on the field and one to the seats. So, after two innings the score is Jays 0, Rays 0, bucket 7, fans 7. This, of course, is not the correct way to keep score. It's just a system I came up with to keep track of friends lost. The only score that matters at the end of the game is the one between the Jays and the Rays.

I'm sure (or almost sure) each team has an accountant who uses a ball tracking system similar to my scoring method. He needs to know if the team will need to buy more balls before the season ends. Just imagine the Rays or your favorite team is in the middle of a playoff push and has used all of their baseballs.

"Oh, no! What will we do?" Answer...send the accountant to the stadium gift shop to buy all the "pearls." Once they are rubbed, they are ready to play. Now, someone call Costa Rica. Fast!

A Ball's Game:
The Ball Talks

Innings 3 and 4

The third and fourth innings go by without any runs being scored. There are also no hits. Both teams made incredible defensive plays to rob batters of potential hits.

There was an epic pitcher versus batter-duel. The batter fouled eight consecutive fastballs into the seats. I love that guy. Eight of my buddies each found a home thanks to that player's one "at bat." He finally struck out looking at a curve ball he didn't think was a strike. Ump said, "Strike three. You're out!" End of argument.

Mid-Game

This is the point in the game where things usually start to happen. By things, I mean hits and runs. The batters are coming to bat for their second or third time against the same pitcher. After seeing a pitcher several times, batters have a better idea of what to look for and start making adjustments. Knowing what the pitcher throws results in greater offensive production. Something big is going to happen this inning. I can feel it.

"Now batting. . ." That voice over the speakers, it's. . . it's a girl! Joan Jett, to be more precise. To be at a game being announced by someone of her fame, I feel honored. The fifth inning quickly vanishes away, as does the voice of Joan Jett. Her guest appearance as the game announcer only lasts one inning. She needs to save her voice for the concert after the game.

A Ball's Game:
The Ball Talks

The sixth inning yields more of the same. The game score is still 0 to 0. The only thing close to producing a run was Kevin's long foul trip. There have been no hits by either team to this point. There have been many defensive gems, robbing batters of potential hits. Several players are wearing a badge of honor of grass and clay stains on their uniforms, proving their efforts. People (fans) can applaud a great defensive play, but you can't cheer for them.

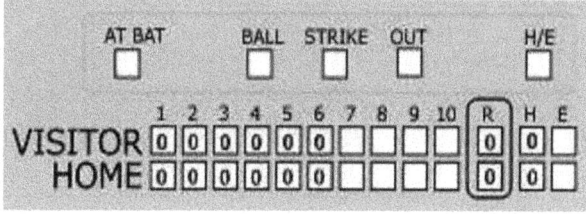

The Stretch

The seventh-inning stretch occurs in the middle of the inning. When is the middle of the inning? It is after the visiting team bats at the top of the inning and before the home team bats in the bottom. This is a time dedicated to the fans. It's your chance to stand up and. . . well. . . stretch. In a game with lots of hits and runs, you may have been standing up for a long time already. Not this game. Score 0 to 0. Hits 0 to 0.

The seventh-inning stretch is a tradition as old as baseball. To get the blood pumping back into your legs, a good stretch needs a little dance. And everyone knows a dance needs a song. What song should we sing? Hmm. How about the one that goes "♪♪ . . . for it's one, two, three strikes, you're out! At the old ball game." "Ladies and gentlemen please join Rock and Roll Hall of Famer Joan Jett in singing "Take Me Out to the Ball Game." Yeah, that's the song I was thinking about. Everyone sing it!

A Ball's Game:
The Ball Talks

"🎵🎵 . . . Take me out to the ball game, take me out to the crowd. Buy me some peanuts and Cracker Jacks. I don't care if I never get back. Let me root, root, root for the home team. If they don't win it's a shame. For it's one, two, three strikes you're out! At the old ball game."

The whole Trop is a giant rock concert. The Rays are going to bust this game wide open in their half of the inning

That was only wishful thinking. The Rays batters go down in three straight strikeouts. Not even hitting a foul ball. This game has been a pitchers' duel.

Two Left

It's the eighth inning. Two are left, unless the score is tied after nine, and we have to go extra innings. Based on the rate we are going through baseballs, we may need more if the game goes to extra innings.

The Jays are batting in the top half of the inning, with two outs. The home plate umpire has just tossed "the General" to the pitcher. I'm going to shout some words of encouragement to him. "Avoid the bats! Avoid the bats!" The pitcher winds up and releases the General towards the plate. "Strike one," yells the ump. The General was a fastball strike. Here he comes again. "Strike two!"

"That's it, General. Show'em your stuff." If he lasts one more strike, he'll have a chance to go home off a Rays bat. CRACK! The sound of the bat hitting the General is as loud as a sonic boom. He has been hit extremely hard. He's going to have a knot on his head the size of a--- well, a baseball. He is flying toward seating

A Ball's Game:
The Ball Talks

section 345. Section 345 is one of the highest fair territory places in the stadium. There are seven rows of seats in the section, rows A thru G. Row A is closest to the fence, four hundred feet from home plate. Row G is furthest from home plate at about four hundred fifty feet. And there are twenty-six seats per row. Seats 1 - 24 are in foul territory. Seats numbered 25 and 26 are fair, barely.

Now you have an idea of the General's flight path. He appears to be traveling in a straight line. "Hook foul, General. Hook foul. Help! Someone, help. Someone catch the General before he goes out of the stadium." Yes! Someone caught the General. It's a guy wearing a Rays jersey and glasses. The guy is Stefan Mathis and he's sitting in section 345, row G, seat 26. Yes! But no! No! That means the General is in fair territory. He has just become a Blue Jays home run. In fact, the longest home run ever hit at Tropicana Field. The General is the first run of the ball game. He is also the first hit of the game, breaking up a double no-hitter we had going.

The next batter strikes out, ending the Blue Jays scoring opportunities. The Rays bats fall silent. Three batters up, three down (out). After eight innings of play, the score is Blue Jays 1 and Rays 0.

A Ball's Game:
The Ball Talks

Making A Big Splash

The top of the ninth has the Rays opting for a new pitcher. Joe Maddon feels the Rays cannot afford to give up another run to the Blue Jays. The Rays send their top relief pitcher to the mound. If anyone can keep the Blue Jays from scoring, this guy can. This guy can throw the ball extremely fast. His philosophy on pitching is this: I'm going to throw the ball as fast as possible. Good luck trying to hit it.

He quickly retires the best Blue Jays batters. Three up and three down. And he did so in legendary fashion. Each Jays batter broke bats trying to get around on his fastball. One broke two bats! He broke one on a foul ball. Batting practice bucket, poor fellow. And then, three weakly hit balls that the Rays defense turned into outs. The mighty timbers wielded by the Blue Jays, reduced to match sticks.

As the Rays hustle into the dugout, Joe says, "Okay, boys! It's now or never." This is the last chance for the Rays to get some runs.

Score or it's over. The Blue Jays have called upon their relief ace to save this game for them. He sits down the first two Rays hitters in quick succession. Two outs. The home plate umpire has signaled a ball boy to bring him some balls. There are two of us left in the R box. Bill and me, Bennie. We were put in the umpire's ball pouch. Excuse me...ball bag. After eight and a half innings you should be up on your baseball lingo. The umpire tells another ball boy to quickly go rub a dozen more balls. I hope the kid knows a dozen is twelve. Bill is the first one pulled out of the bag. I hope Bill does not become a one ball out. If that happens, game over, Blue Jays win. Then I'll be put back into the R box awaiting the next home game, which won't be for another twelve days. After today's game, the Rays have a day off. Actually, it's travel day. Then the Rays begin a ten-game west coast road trip. I'll be left in that R box for twelve days. That's enough time for me to become a general; maybe a general with two or three stars.

A Ball's Game:
The Ball Talks

The pitcher winds up and releases the pitch. Here comes Bill. He's a curve ball. "Break, Bill. Break! Watch out! You're about to hit the batter." KERPLUNK!! Bill has hit the batter. Bill was a curve ball that didn't break. Kerplunk is a sound you don't want to hear in a baseball game. Crack is the sound of the bat hitting a ball. And that's good, if you're a bat, of course. Kerplunk, not so good. That sound means a ball has hit a batting helmet. When a pitcher hits a batter, the batter is awarded first base. Anyone on base (a base runner) has the potential to come around to score a run.

The batter shakes off the pain of being hit with a baseball and makes his way to first base. Bill lies in the dirt at home plate. The umpire looks at the blue streak on Bill's cover. The blue streak comes from Bill's collision with the Rays batting helmet. Bill is thrown to a ball girl, destined for the bucket. I hope Bill's appearance in the game has not been in vain.

The umpire pulls me out of his ball bag. He quickly inspects me and then tosses me to the pitcher. The pitcher gives me a little extra rubbing while contemplating his mistake of hitting the batter with the previous pitch.

Meanwhile, over the speakers, we hear, "Now batting, third baseman Evan Longoria." He's one of the Rays' best hitters. They refer to him around the clubhouse as "Longo," but I don't know why.

Through a slit in the pitcher's glove, I see the catcher has signaled for me to be a fastball. Here I come towards the plate at ninety-five miles per hour. Longo swings and misses. Strike one! The catcher signals for the same thing. Again, Longo swings and misses. Strike two! The Rays are down to their last strike. In an effort to fool the batter, the catcher wants a curve ball this time.

As I fly towards the plate, I look like a fastball. Suddenly I make a sharp break to the left. If Longo swings he will surely miss me. But he doesn't, and I miss the strike zone. Ball one. The catcher signals for another fastball. The pitcher shakes his head no. The pitcher would like to throw a different type of pitch.

A Ball's Game:
The Ball Talks

The catcher puts down two fingers. The pitcher agrees. Again, I approach the plate and make a sharp break. Longo doesn't swing. I'm too far outside to be a strike and too high to hit. Ball two. The catcher wants another curve ball. Three times lucky is what they say. This time as I come to the plate I don't break at all. I almost hit Longo. Ball three.

For a fourth time the catcher signals for a curve. The pitcher agrees. What kind of pitcher with a count of three balls and two strikes, two outs in the bottom of the ninth, throws a curve? He can not afford to walk Longo, putting another man on base. Three straight curve balls have been balls. He's protecting a one run lead, with the possible tying run on first. Longo represents the go ahead and winning run if he were to come around the bases to score.

What kind of guy throws a curve in this situation? This guy, of course. He is the American League save leader. He has the ability to throw the right pitch at the right time. The three straight balls do not worry him. He can throw every pitch in his arsenal for a strike any time, in any situation. The pitcher stares down Longo at the plate, adding to the pressure, then starts his wind-up.

Here I come, curve ball number four. I'm coming towards the plate, curving...slowly. Longo grips the bat tightly and swings with all his might. CRACK! "Ouch!" I've been hit very hard, and right on the bottom. I leave the bat like a rocket. I'm flying very high. And as hard as I've been hit, I believe I'm going to go very far. Based on my quick calculations, my trajectory has me headed toward the rays tank in the right-center field.

A Ball's Game:
The Ball Talks

Timeout. Please stop the action. You don't know about the rays tank? The rays tank is a ten thousand-gallon aquarium just beyond the right-center field fence. It is full of rays, which are small, flat, disk-shaped marine animals that can swim very fast. During the game, fans can go into the aquarium area to feed the rays. Don't worry. They don't bite. By the way, since I am about to land in the rays tank, there is something you need to know---I can't swim!

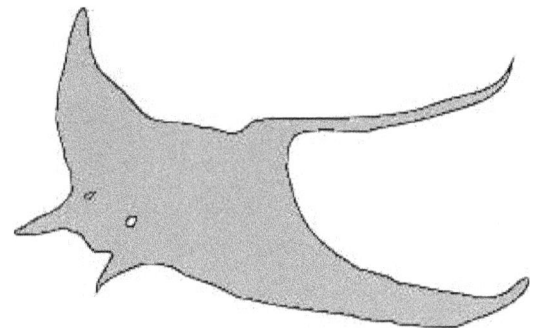

Before I make a splash down, I'm going to tell you a quick story. Don't worry. It won't take long. The average Major League game lasts three hours and twenty-two minutes. We've got plenty of time. Before 2008, the

Tampa Bay Rays were known as the Devil Rays. Devil rays are large menacing looking creatures that patrol the depths of the ocean. They look sort of like a bat. No. Not a baseball bat. The furry wings, sharp teeth, beady eyes, scary face kind of bat.

These monsters of the deep swim the waters of the Gulf of Mexico. Hence the connection between Tampa Bay and devil rays. Some thought a team with the word "Devil" in its name would strike fear into the hearts of their opponents.

In order to pay tribute to the Devil Rays, the Tampa Bay baseball organization put an aquarium inside the stadium. The aquarium is stocked with the much smaller cousins of devil rays. A full-grown devil ray can be twenty feet wide, ten to twelve feet long, and weigh in excess of a thousand pounds.

In 2008 the "Devil" part of the name was dropped. The team became the Tampa Bay Rays. And for the first time in franchise history, they made it to the playoffs. The newly

A Ball's Game:
The Ball Talks

renamed team made it all the way to the World Series. They have been a good team since the name change, with several playoff appearances.

Back to live action. Where was I? High in the air, mid-flight, about to make a watery landing. I should close my eyes and mouth. Saltwater tastes bad and burns your eyes. I wonder if salt water will wash off my mud, turning me back into a pearl.

I can't look. I close my eyes as I quickly fall toward my splash down. 3, 2, 1 ... Smack! Smack?

Wait! That's not the sound of a ball hitting the water. That's the sound of...of a ball hitting a leather glove. The Trop erupts in a thunderous roar. I have been saved from immersion by a little girl stretching her pink glove over the rays tank.

Being caught by a pink glove means three things. First, I have not been caught by the Blue Jays center fielder. Second, I'm going home. No batting practice bucket for me. And finally... The Rays win! The dome of Tropicana Field will glow orange tonight. The orange glow lets residents of the area know their Rays have won today's game. If you see what looks like a giant orange when you are flying into or out of the Tampa Bay area, you'll know the reason. If "The Trop" is not lit up, let's hope the Rays are on a road trip. I'm a two-run game-winning home run. I'm a hero. Bill too. His contribution was putting the game-tying runner on base.

Evan Longoria will be the hero of today's game to the fans. I will be the hero to the little girl. And, Bill, the hero of the bucket. The

A Ball's Game:
The Ball Talks

parts we balls and those bats play in the course of a game are often downplayed. Oh, well. At least we had fun.

I hear a woman's voice say, "Great catch, Lucy." A man says, "Way to go, girl!" These are Lucy's parents. Through a slot between the fingers of the pink baseball glove, I can see a name written on the glove: Lucy Martin. I've been caught by a girl named Lucy.

Everyone in the stadium is cheering. A loud horn is blasting. The scoreboard is flashing a message... Rays win, Rays win, Rays win. All of the Rays players are congratulating Longo as he touches home plate. The whole stadium is one big, loud celebration.

My flight and catch are being replayed on the stadium video screen. Just before I hit the water, my hero, Lucy, catches me. Seated in stadium section 150, Lucy stretched her glove as far as she could to grab me. I looked like a scoop of vanilla ice cream sitting on top of a cone. A pink cone, at that. Lucy's catch over the water will surely be ESPN's top play of the day.

"Come on, Lucy. We have to get Longo to sign that ball," says her dad. Lucy, her dad, and I make our way through the cheering crowds to the Rays clubhouse.

"Thank you for coming to today's game," says the game announcer. "Today's attendance is 22,412. Time of game . . . three hours, eleven minutes. For those of you waiting on the Joan Jett concert, please make your way down to field-level seats while the stage is set up in center field. The concert will begin in thirty minutes. For those of you leaving the stadium, please drive carefully and come again."

Lucy, her dad, and I arrive at the Rays clubhouse. A throng of fans are getting autographs from the Rays players. Players are signing hats, balls, bats, gloves, books, programs, anything that can be marked with an autograph. One player even signed someone's shoe. Here comes Evan Longoria. Everyone is shouting. "Longo, tell us about the

A Ball's Game:
The Ball Talks

home run." "Longo, sign my book." "Longo, sign my jersey." "Longo, sign my forearm." Longo this, Longo that. Longo, Longo, Longo.

In her little hand, Lucy holds me up in the air. "Mr. Longoria, here's your ball," she says.

"Are you the little girl who made that amazing catch on my home run?" asks Longoria.

"Yes, sir," Lucy answers shyly.

"This is your ball, young lady. You earned it," says Evan. "May I sign your ball, miss?"

"Yes, sir," she replies. Evan Longoria takes me in his hands and signs his autograph on my cover. Under his name, he adds the words...What a Catch!

"At this time please welcome to the stage Joan Jett and the Heartbreakers," we hear over the p.a.

"Thank you, Mr. Longoria," says Lucy's dad.

"My pleasure," says Longoria.

"We have to hurry, Lucy. The concert is about to start," quips her dad. We (my best friend Lucy and I), with her dad in tow, run back to the field. A stadium usher lets us on to the field so we can be close to the action. We nudge our way through the crowd until we are standing next to the stage.

"I'm so glad to be here today at beautiful Tropicana Field. Wasn't that a great game?" asks Joan Jett. The crowd cheers. And then it starts..."I saw him dancing there by the record machine...I love rock and roll." Lucy is dancing to the beat of the song. She is waving me in one hand, the pink glove in the other.

After one song, the music stops. Joan Jett has recognized me, the pink glove, and Lucy. She invites us up on the stage. The crowd cheers wildly as we come onto the stage. Everyone recognizes us. If you did not see the catch in live-action, you've at least seen the video replay by now. We're celebrities. Ever since "The Catch" was made, it has been shown on the scoreboard at least fifty times while the stage was being prepared.

A Ball's Game:
The Ball Talks

Joan Jett asks, "What's your name, little girl?"

"Lucy."

"May I sign your ball, Lucy?"

"Yes. I would love that," says Lucy. Lucy hands me to Ms. Jett. One of her Blackheart band members gives a pen to Joan and she autographs my leather cover..."Joan Jett" and under her name, "You rock, girl."

Lucy is going to be the envy of all her family and friends. Some of them may have a Major League ball, although it is highly unlikely. Even if they do, it's not signed like me. One side of my cover has the autograph of a Hall of Famer, and the other side a very likely future inductee.

Home Sweet Home

It has been a few years since that wonderful day. I now sit in a prominent place at Lucy's house, encased in a clear acrylic box for everyone to see. Everyone who comes into the house hears the story of Lucy's amazing catch. The part about the autographs and the concert are also included in the story. The day rock and roll and baseball joined forces will long be remembered by this family.

The End

www.ingramcontent.com/pod-product-compliance
Lightning Source LLC
LaVergne TN
LVHW050137080526
838202LV00061B/6508